From whichever direction you look at it, Durham Cathedral is a stunning sight. At first there can seem something forbidding about it, but its splendour is a welcoming splendour, and this is appropriate for a place that exists primarily for Christian worship. Worship is our 'core activity', and it has been so since the tenth century, when a few monks fleeing from Viking raiders brought the remains of St Cuthbert to this place and made it their home. Without Cuthbert there would have been no Cathedral; but that does not make the cult of Cuthbert the Cathedral's sole purpose.

As time went by the Cathedral became a place of sanctuary from those fleeing the law; they would grasp hold of the Sanctuary Knocker and claim the right to enter and stay while they organised their affairs. After a certain period they had to decide whether to stand trial or to flee the country.

The right of sanctuary was abolished in English law in 1623, but the Cathedral remains a place of quiet and prayer, where all people are encouraged to enter and take time to think about their lives in the light, not so much of the law of England, as of the Gospel of Jesus Christ.

Co

Left ~ Replica of the Sanctuary Knocker. The original is in the Treasures of St Cuthbert

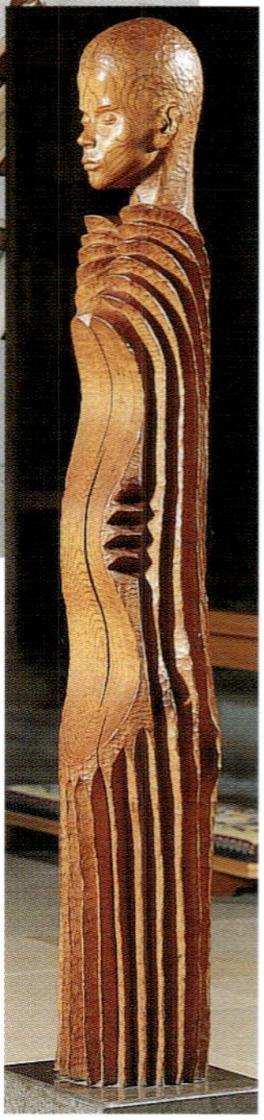

The building of Durham Cathedral was begun in the late eleventh century as a shrine for the body of St Cuthbert. After the monks arrived with his body, they built a temporary church. This was succeeded by what became known as the 'White Church', which was begun in 996 and completed in 1017. The foundation stone of the present Cathedral was laid in 1093, after William the Conqueror had introduced a community of Benedictine monks here in succession to the Anglo-Saxon community to which Cuthbert had belonged.

We have the Venerable Bede to thank for everything we know about Cuthbert. Bede was a monk at Jarrow, about fifteen miles (24km) to the north of Durham, towards the mouth of the River Tyne; and he was one of the most

Above and left ~ *The Galilee Chapel, showing the thirteenth-century wall paintings*
Left inset ~ Annunciation
Right ~ *A page from Bede's* Life of Cuthbert

learned men of his day. Bede is buried here, in the Galilee Chapel; the tomb of Cuthbert is at the east end of the Cathedral. Cuthbert was renowned for his goodness, and Bede was distinguished by his pursuit of the truth. Between them runs the length of the Cathedral, a symbol of beauty holding together the other two principal virtues of truth and goodness. Durham Cathedral is an image in stone of the relationship between the three.

The beautiful, light Galilee Chapel was begun in the twelfth century, after the main part of the Cathedral. It is so named because the great procession that ended the Sunday service would finish here, and this symbolised the return of Jesus to Galilee after the Resurrection, as related in some of the Gospel accounts. The stained glass windows of Cuthbert and some other saints serve as a reminder that all the saints of God are people through whom the light of God shines. Cuthbert's Coffin is the one in which he was buried eleven years after his death, when the monks discovered that his body had not decomposed in the grave; his Pectoral Cross was discovered around his neck when the grave was excavated in 1827.

Epistola sci Bede.
DOMINO
sanctissimo
ac beatissimo
patri eadfrido
epo. sed et omni congregationi fratrum qui in lin
disfarnensi insula xpo deseruiunt. beda fide
lis uester salutem. Quia iussistis dilectissimi ut
libro quem de uita beate memorie patris nostri
cuthberti uestro rogatu composui. prefationem
aliquam in fronte iuxta morem prefigerem. per quam
legentibus uniuersis et uestre uoluntatis deside
rium. et obedientie nostre pariter assensio fraterna
clarescere: placuit in capite prefationis et uo
bis qui nostis ad memoriam reuocare. et eis qui
ignorant hec forte legentibus notum facere. quia
nec sine certissima exquisitione rerum gesta
rum aliquid de tanto uiro scribere. nec tan
dem ea que scripseram sine subtili exami
natione testium indubiorum passim transcri

The manuscript of Bede's *Life of Cuthbert* illustrates the connection between the goodness of Cuthbert and the learning of Bede. It also highlights one of the functions of the Cathedral when it was a priory: to study and disseminate the Christian gospel by word, action and text. All these items are on display in the exhibition on the Treasures of St Cuthbert, just off the Cathedral Cloisters, and a fuller *Guide* to them is available there.

As you enjoy the light and peace of this Chapel, you may wish to note the wall paintings above the arches. They date from the thirteenth century and show elements of the story of the Crucifixion of Jesus; you should be able to make out a cross, the tools of the soldiers who executed Jesus and the ladder used for removing his body from the cross.

The statue in the middle of the Galilee Chapel is entitled *Annunciation*, by Joseph Pyrz. It recalls the story in St Luke's Gospel of the visit of the angel Gabriel to Mary to tell her that she was to be the mother of Christ. The serenity of her face speaks of faith, and its many-faceted aspect subverts conventional distinctions of race. Here is Everywoman, pregnant with the Son of God.

Left ~ *St Cuthbert's Coffin and Pectoral Cross*

The Galilee is also the Cathedral's Lady Chapel, that is, the chapel devoted to the Blessed Virgin Mary. When the building of a Lady Chapel was begun at the east end of the Cathedral, the foundations were insecure, and the walls began to crack. This was taken as a sign that Cuthbert would not tolerate women near his shrine, so the chapel was moved to the west end. The suggestion that Cuthbert disliked women is unfounded, for he was on good terms with, for example, St Hild of Whitby, as well as other Christian women of his day; it would appear that the monks may have been attributing their own prejudices to Cuthbert himself.

Behind the Altar are wall paintings; the one reproduced here is of a bishop, generally thought to be Cuthbert; he carries a hooked staff, or crook, for he is regarded as a shepherd in the Church, with a desire to seek out the lost. The imagery comes from the passage in St John's Gospel, chapter 10, where Jesus refers to himself as 'the good shepherd'. The painting facing the bishop on the wall is thought to be of St Oswald, King of Northumbria; however, we cannot be completely certain of either of these subjects.

Above left ~ The Galilee Chapel
Above right ~ Wall painting in the Chapel

In the Nave of the Cathedral a large number of columns support the roof; here in the Galilee the columns are lighter (for the roof is neither as high nor as heavy), and there is a sense of lightness. The dog-tooth carving on the arches represents the work of a slightly later time than the main part of the Cathedral, when ornamentation of the basic Romanesque design was becoming popular. It adds to the delicate nature of the stonework.

The Venerable Bede, whose tomb is here, was a young man when Cuthbert was Bishop. He wrote biblical commentaries, works of scientific exploration, and a number of other works; it was largely through his influence that the change in the reckoning of the years was brought about that gave us BC, 'before Christ', and AD, *Anno Domini*, Latin for 'in the year of our Lord'. His *History of the English Church and People* remains one of our chief sources for the history of the period. His remains were brought here in 1022 by a zealous – some would say overzealous – sacrist named Alfred Westoe.

Bede's Tomb is simple, and part of its inscription is reproduced here; the Latin means 'in this grave lie the bones of the Venerable Bede'.

The Tomb stands here as a reminder of the value of learning, not only in this University city, but also to all who come to visit. Alongside his great learning, Bede cultivated a love of Jesus Christ, and the words from his commentary on the Book of Revelation, in the New Testament, indicate something of the depth of his spirituality. The window shown here was designed to commemorate the 1300th anniversary of Bede's birth *circa* 672.

The large tomb against the west door of the Cathedral is that of Cardinal Thomas Langley. He was Bishop of Durham in the first part of the fifteenth century. He was a popular bishop who did much to develop both the life of the Cathedral and its beauty. He is remembered each year in November as the founder of Durham School, part of his legacy to the city as one committed to the education of its people.

Right ~ Bede Window
Left ~ Bede's Tomb
Below ~ Part of the inscription from Bede's Tomb

Left ~ The St Cuthbert service in the Nave
Right ~ The West Window

Not for nothing did the writer Bill Bryson call Durham Cathedral 'the finest building on planet earth'. Nevertheless, the view of the Nave pictured here tells only half the story. This is the earliest example of rib vaulting in Europe, and contained within the outer walls are the first flying buttresses.

No plans were drawn up for the design of the building; the master builder saw in his mind the finished project he desired and shared his vision with the craftsmen. A wooden scaffold was constructed, and the stones were built up against it, so forming the elegant Norman arches. When each arch was complete, the master builder would himself knock away the scaffolding supports. If the arch fell, another master builder would be needed as well as more scaffolding.

The builder's vision is a metaphor for hope, his skill is a parable of faith, and his commitment to seeing the task through to completion is an example of love. The famous Christian triad of faith, hope and love is brought together in St Paul's first letter to the Corinthians, chapter 13. This triad is not a remote theory; its three concepts inform the very way people conduct their lives and carry out their work.

Christian life begins with baptism, and at the west end of the Cathedral, just by the entrance, stands the font, in which baptism takes place. This huge marble font dates from the time of John Cosin, who was a Canon here during the reign of Charles I, then Bishop under Charles II in the seventeenth century. The two reigns were separated by the Civil War and the period of the Commonwealth, when Oliver Cromwell ruled the country as Lord Protector.

Cosin was a brilliant man who played a part in the development of the Book of Common Prayer. He also worked hard to beautify the Cathedral after the austere period of the Commonwealth,

when a sober moral piety took precedence over the vibrant and colourful celebration of the joy of God in the faith of the nation.

The Font Cover dates from the same period, its ornate decoration clearly an attempt to emphasise the significance of baptism in the life of the Church and of the believer. On the very top of the cover is the form of a bird, presumably a dove, to represent the Holy Spirit of God, who descended on Jesus at his baptism.

The Organ Case dates from the latter half of the seventeenth century. It was part of the screen that divided the Quire from the Nave but was placed in its present position in the late nineteenth century, the instrument having been removed some years earlier.

Above and right ~ The Font and Cover, with detail of the top of the Cover

The West Window, pictured here, dates from 1867. It depicts the story of the family of Jesse, the father of the biblical King David. According to St Matthew's Gospel, chapter 1, Jesus was descended from this line. There are seven lights in the window, containing twenty-one figures. Jesse is at the bottom of the light in the centre, and the branches of the family tree all stem from him.

Around the figure of Christ in the arms of the Virgin Mary are three images: 'the lamb of God', the Annunciation, and the Adoration of the Magi.

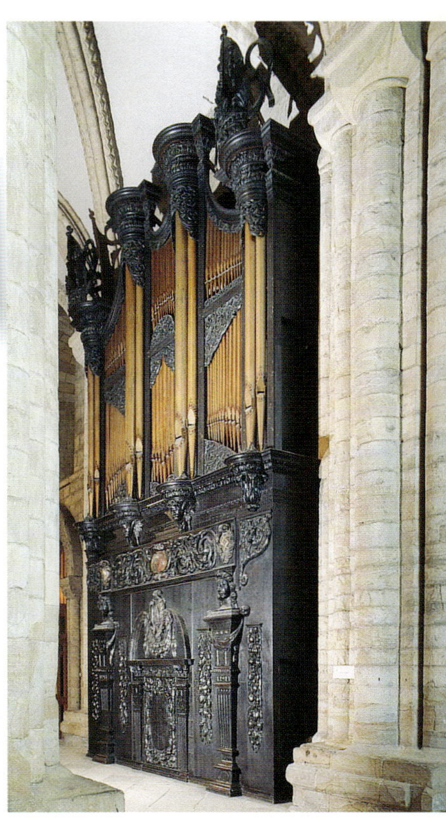

Above ~ The Organ Case

The Miners' Memorial, a monument of particular poignancy and ambiguity, was installed in 1947. Until recently mining was the major industry of County Durham. Generations of families worked the mines, and whole communities depended upon the yield of coal that they produced. However, that production was not without its cost. The Memorial, along with the Book of Remembrance and the Safety Lamp, serve as reminders of those who died in the mining industry. Nevertheless, and on the other hand, the closure of the pits was a bitter blow both to the economy and to the community life of the county. All these ambivalent feelings are registered in these reminders of the mining industry in County Durham.

The Neville Chantry reminds us of another way in which the Cathedral – and the Priory before it – was involved in the life of the community. The Neville family were generous benefactors of the Cathedral in the late medieval period, and their gifts included exceedingly generous donations of fabric, plate and ornaments. In 1416 a Chantry Chapel was built to receive the bodies of John, Lord Neville, and his wife, Lady Alice. A sum of money was left to enable Masses to be said for them each day. Their statues, which were mutilated either during the Reformation or the Civil War of the seventeenth century, lie in the place that they once occupied within the chapel that was built for them.

The Rose Window is just over ninety-eight feet (30m) in circumference and was completed in the early years of the nineteenth century. It shows Christ, 'the Saviour of the World', as the inscription says (though it cannot be seen with the naked eye), surrounded by the twelve apostles and the twenty-four 'elders' from the Book of Revelation, chapter 4. On either side of the window are two rows of Durham's bishops, priors and deans.

The Nave of the Cathedral is the place where the whole people of God gather for worship. The word 'nave' means 'ship', and two images are called to mind here. The first speaks of the shape and size of the building that contains all the people. (If it were upside down, the roof would form the hull.) The second image recalls the story of Noah's ark, which was the 'ship' in which Noah and his family were kept safe during the Flood. In the same way the whole human race is welcomed into the house of God; and all people are 'saved' by God from sin. Crowds gather in the Cathedral on a number of occasions: for Christmas carol services; for the Miners' Gala service, for the service for the Courts of Justice; and for regular Sunday worship.

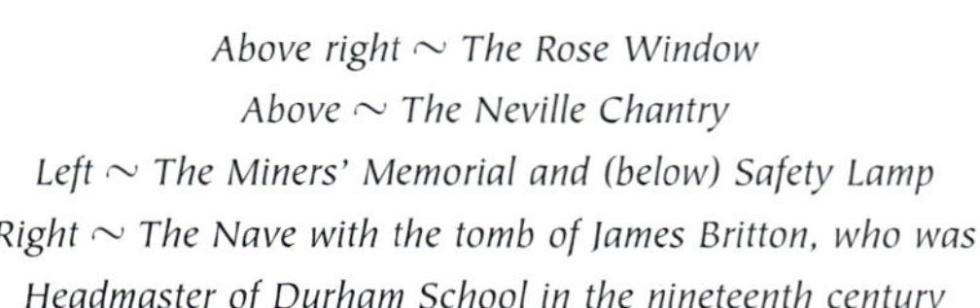

Above right ~ The Rose Window
Above ~ The Neville Chantry
Left ~ The Miners' Memorial and (below) Safety Lamp
Right ~ The Nave with the tomb of James Britton, who was Headmaster of Durham School in the nineteenth century

Left ~ *Prior Castell's Clock*
Below ~ The Te Deum *window*

The splendid clock in the South Transept was installed by Thomas Castell, who became Prior of the community at the end of the fifteenth century. The number of monks had fallen to around forty when he was elected, but he was an energetic leader who did much to improve the fortunes of the Cathedral. He not only had this clock installed, but also added to the Cathedral's lands and rebuilt the gateway to what is now the College, where the Cathedral clergy and other staff live. The Clock shows not only the time of day, but also the day of the month and the phases of the moon.

The Clock has seen many changes. The community existed for nearly the first 500 years of its life as a priory, with up to eighty monks in its heyday. At the Reformation during the 1540s the Priory was dissolved and the monks dispersed. The Prior was made the first Dean of the 'newly founded' Cathedral, and twelve monks

Left ~ *Bishop Barrington's memorial*

Right ~ The Durham Light Infantry Chapel
Below ~ Regimental colours

were appointed as Canons and members of the Chapter. (The Cathedral was thereafter known as one 'of the new foundation'; 'new' dates back to the Reformation.)

The *Te Deum* window was unveiled in 1869 in memory of Archdeacon Charles Thorp, who was one of the chief advocates for the founding of the University of Durham and who became its first Warden. Various saints are depicted in the window and the opening words of the ancient Christian hymn, the *Te Deum*, are also included: 'We praise thee, O God; we acknowledge thee to be the Lord'.

The Durham Light Infantry Chapel was dedicated in 1924 to commemorate County Durham's own regiment. The Books of Remembrance list the names of those who fell in battle.

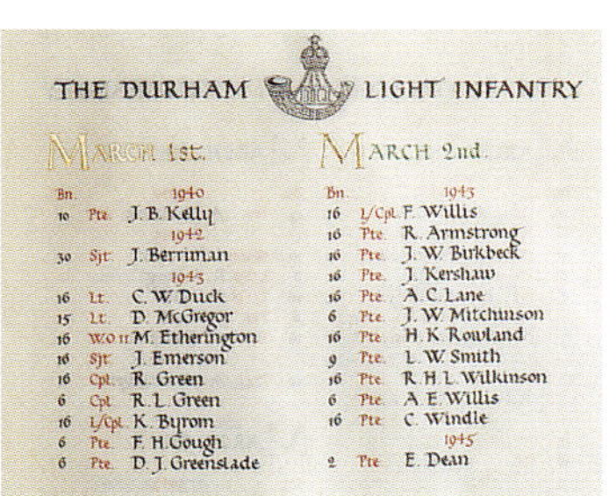

The memorial to Bishop Shute Barrington commemorates a well-loved Bishop at the end of the eighteenth and the beginning of the nineteenth century. He was renowned for his generosity and support for mining communities.

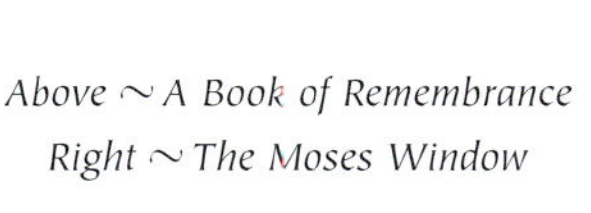

THE DURHAM LIGHT INFANTRY

Bn.		March 1st.	Bn.		March 2nd.
		1940			1943
10	Pte.	J. B. Kelly	16	L/Cpl.	F. Willis
		1942	16	Pte.	R. Armstrong
30	Sjt.	J. Berriman	16	Pte.	J. W. Birkbeck
		1943	16	Pte.	J. Kershaw
16	Lt.	C. W. Duck	16	Pte.	A. C. Lane
15	Lt.	D. McGregor	6	Pte.	J. W. Mitchinson
16	W.O.II	M. Etherington	16	Pte.	H. K. Rowland
16	Sjt.	J. Emerson	9	Pte.	L. W. Smith
16	Cpl.	R. Green	16	Pte.	R. H. L. Wilkinson
6	Cpl.	R. L. Green	6	Pte.	A. E. Willis
16	L/Cpl.	K. Byrom	16	Pte.	C. Windle
6	Pte.	F. H. Gough			1945
6	Pte.	D. J. Greenslade	2	Pte.	E. Dean

The Moses Window is so named because it depicts a detail of the life of Moses, who, according to the Letter to the Hebrews, 'refused to be called a son of Pharaoh's daughter'. The window shows him leaving the court of Pharaoh having chosen to suffer with his own people, the Israelites, rather than enjoy the pleasures of the Egyptian court. The window was designed by Henry Holiday, a friend of William Holman Hunt and Edward Burne-Jones.

Above ~ A Book of Remembrance
Right ~ The Moses Window

Above ~ The Central Tower from the Crossing
Left ~ The Central Tower

You need a head for heights to climb the 325 steps to the Tower, but the ascent is well worth the effort. Once you have reached the top the views are magnificent – both inside and outside the Cathedral. The present Tower was completed around 1490, after its predecessor had been destroyed by lightning and fire sixty years earlier. It houses the bells, the oldest three of which date from 1693. They were rehung in 1980, and the ninth and tenth bells were added at that time.

The photograph of the Quire reveals the symmetry of its floor, as well as the lush scarlet of the furnishings and the brightness of the organ pipes.

Looking up into the lantern from the crossing is also a heady experience; the height up into the lantern is 154 feet (47m). This is also a good point from which to look westwards up the Nave. The beautifully carved columns were prepared away from the building site – like the Temple at Jerusalem in the Old Testament – and installed here in order. The harmony of the building relies in part on the fact that the circumference of the columns is equal to their height: over twenty-one feet (6.5m).

The Screen, Pulpit and Lectern are by George Gilbert Scott and date from the 1870s. The Lectern was the subject of some controversy in the 1930s, for many people did not like it. A decision was taken to remove it to the Chapel of the Nine Altars, but it was restored to its proper place in 1991.

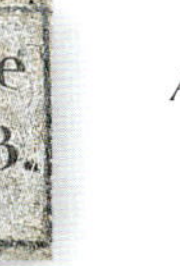

Above right ~ The Quire seen from above the Crossing
Left ~ The Tower Staircase and inscription

LLITE PUERI SAPIENTER

Left ~ The Bishop's Throne and Bishop Hatfield's Tomb
Below left ~ Detail of Bishop Hatfield's Tomb
Below right ~ The Millennium Pulpit Fall

This full-page picture of the Quire conveys something of its splendour. The back rows of the choir stalls were commissioned by John Cosin, who also installed the Font at the west end (see page 7). His work of making the Cathedral more attractive included improving the music of the Cathedral, as well as the place where it was sung. The carving on the stalls is intricate, and the misericords show a wide variety of beasts and other figures, who all join here in the praise of God. An illustration of the end of one of the rows of the choir stalls indicates the detail with which those Restoration craftsmen went about their task of beautifying this house of God.

The Pulpit dates from the same period, and the embroidered Fall from its reading desk was a gift from the Cathedral Broderers to mark the start of the third millennium. It was designed by Leonard Childs and depicts the four symbols of the Gospels: the man representing St Matthew, the lion representing St Mark, the ox representing St Luke and the eagle representing St John.

The tomb of Bishop Thomas Hatfield lies under the Bishop's Throne. It is said that Hatfield decided that Bishops of Durham deserved a throne at least as high as that of the Bishop of Rome – the Pope. The decoration of shrine and throne are intricate and beautiful; one of the carvings is illustrated here on this page. Bishop Michael Ramsey used to say that he was the only person in the Cathedral who could look out from his seat and see the world.

Regular worship takes place in the Quire, with morning prayer to start the working day of the clergy, and evening prayer to conclude it; the latter is usually sung daily (except Mondays) by the Cathedral Choir, which comprises twenty boys and twelve men. The boys receive scholarships from the Chapter to study at the Chorister School, which is situated within the Cathedral grounds.

Left ~ The Quire, looking east
Left inset ~ A pew end in the Quire
Right ~ A misericord in the Quire

The High Altar is the principal place at which the Holy Communion is celebrated. Its location, at the visual centre of the building, marks it out as special. It is here that bread and wine are taken, offered to God and

Above ~ Detail of the Neville Screen
Right ~ The High Altar

shared with the people; and all in order to represent the actions of Jesus on the night when he was betrayed and arrested. These simple actions, for all the dignity and seriousness of the ceremony, speak of the self-giving, sacrificial and passionate love of God for the world of humanity. The intricacy of the carving can be seen in these photographs; such meticulous craftsmanship was considered appropriate for this most holy part of the Cathedral.

In the Middle Ages the ceremony would have been even more elaborate than it is now. It has been suggested that the Reformation marked a change in the religious practice of the people that was imposed by an authoritarian government.

Above ~ Stonework near the High Altar

That might have been so in some parts of the country, but in others, including Durham, there was little objection to the changes that were brought about. There was a mood in the nation that things needed to change; and the Priory at Durham fitted in with the will of both King and people.

Immediately behind the Altar is the Neville Screen, built by the Neville family between 1372 and 1380. Before the Reformation the Screen held 107 statues in its various niches. It is said that these were removed and hidden before the King's Commissioners could come and destroy them; they remain hidden to this day.

The Millennium Window in the South Quire Aisle was designed by Joseph Nuttgens to commemorate the foundation of the Diocese when St Cuthbert's body was brought to Durham in 995. It depicts scenes from the life of the Diocese, from agriculture and mining through to modern industries such as chemicals and car manufacturing.

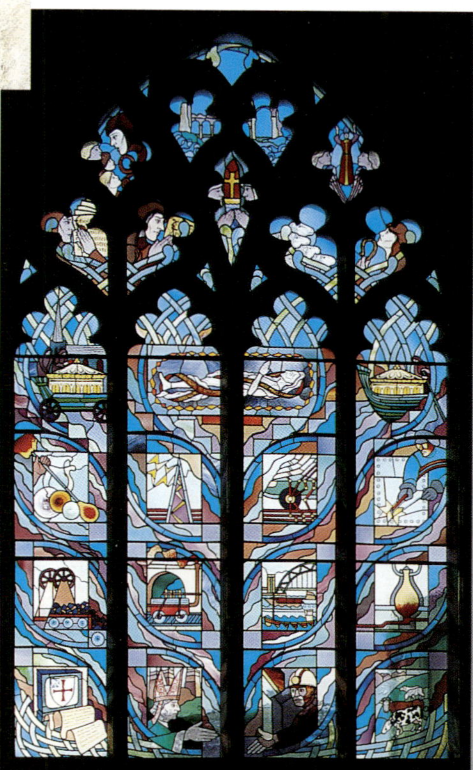

Right ~ Window in the Chapel of the Nine Altars
Below ~ The Millennium Window in the South Quire Aisle

St Cuthbert was Bishop of Lindisfarne, the Diocese covering the north-eastern part of England, in the second half of the seventh century. He was so famous for his goodness and kindness that when he died many people visited his tomb to give thanks for him and to pray, that they might be like him.

He lived the last two years of his life with his community on Lindisfarne (Holy Island), and he was buried there after he had died in his solitary hermitage on Inner Farne in 687. After his burial his tomb so quickly became a destination for pilgrimages that, just eleven years after his death, his coffin was dug up so that it could be elevated in the sight of the pilgrims. The coffin was opened, and the monks were astounded to find not just bones, but the body of Cuthbert – uncorrupted.

In those days the north-east of England was often subject to raids by Viking invaders. Soon after Cuthbert's death these became so frequent that the community of monks left Lindisfarne, carrying his body with them. After several years of travelling around the north of England, they settled in Durham in 995.

The Tester above the tomb was designed by Sir Ninian Comper and added in 1949; it shows Christ in glory, surrounded by the four Evangelists. The statue is of Cuthbert holding the head of St Oswald, the Christian king who supported the preaching of the gospel in Northumbria; the head rests in the same tomb as Cuthbert's body.

Above ~ The tester
Left ~ St Cuthbert's Shrine

Right ~ St Cuthbert carrying St Oswald's head
Below ~ The inscription on St Cuthbert's Tomb

The Chapel of the Nine Altars was built so that all the priests who were members of the Benedictine community could say Mass each day. Now there are just two altars, and another will be completed in the next few years. The Chapter has decided to raise the profile of women saints in the Cathedral, since a number played an important part in its history. St Hild of Whitby was a friend of Cuthbert, and she is commemorated with an icon next to an altar dedicated to her on the north side of the central altar. On the south side will be an altar dedicated to St Margaret of Scotland, who was married to King Malcolm of Scotland, and she is reputed to have been present at the laying of the foundation stone in 1093.

The Chapel was begun in 1242, when Thomas Melsonby was Prior. Thirty days' remission of purgatory was promised to those who contributed towards its completion. The architect was Richard of Farnham, and he brilliantly added a sense of height to the building by lowering the floor while retaining the level of the roof.

The statue shown here is of Bishop William Van Mildert, who with the Dean and Chapter founded the University of Durham in 1832.

There is also shown here a detail of local 'Frosterley Marble', with which the pillars are constructed.

Above ~ Altar Frontal
Above right ~ Altar Frontal detail

Right ~ Memorial to Bishop Van Mildert

Above ~ 'Frosterley Marble', showing characteristic fossils
Right ~ The Chapel of the Nine Altars

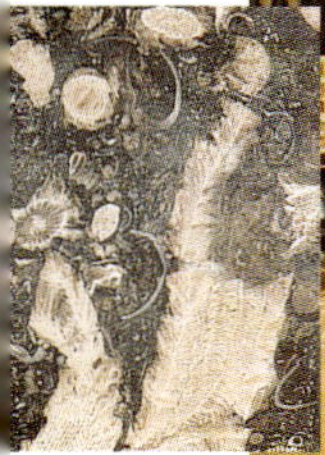

The memorial to Bishop Joseph Lightfoot in the North Quire Aisle commemorates a remarkable scholar. In the latter part of the nineteenth century, he made a major contribution to New Testament study by introducing German biblical scholarship to a sceptical English readership.

The window in the North Transept shows the Virgin and Child and St Cuthbert. On either side are the four Doctors of the Western Church: Jerome, Ambrose, Augustine and Gregory. This window was installed in 1875.

The banner in this Transept is a gift from the Diocese of Lesotho in southern Africa, with which the Durham Diocese is linked. Such a specific link reminds us that the Church is one body of Christians throughout the world.

Above ~ The St Gregory Window in the North Transept
Right ~ View towards the North Transept

The window shown above depicts St Gregory of Nazianzus, one of the 'Cappadocian Fathers' of the late fourth century. He, St Basil of Caesarea, and St Gregory of Nyssa (Basil's younger brother) were all scholar bishops who were fearless in their defence of the Orthodox faith at the Council of Constantinople in 381. The Arians, against whom they argued, taught that Jesus Christ was not fully divine.

The Bedesmen's Benches date from the fourteenth century, when Bishop Walter Skirlaw installed them for old men who received a small pension in return for the benefit of their prayers. Today eight Bedesmen continue the tradition of providing a welcome to all visitors.

Above ~ Bishop Lightfoot's Memorial
Right ~ Detail of the Bedesmen's Benches

In the Cathedral's heyday, in the Middle Ages, the Cloisters would have been the centre of the community's life in between the round of services that the monks attended in the Quire. The scriptorium was situated against the south wall of the Cathedral, so it was here that the monks spent their time studying. Their texts included Canon Law (that is, the law that regulates the life of the Church) along with biblical commentary and theology. It is also said that knowledge of classical literature was better here than in most other places in the country. A number of Durham manuscripts may be seen among the Treasures of St Cuthbert, in the exhibition just off the south-west corner of the Cloisters; the richness of their binding and decoration give some indication of the wealth of the monastery when these texts were produced. The Cloisters were rebuilt during the period 1406–18.

A small fragment of stained glass from the medieval period may be seen in the window of the Chapter House. It is reproduced above to give some indication of the intricacy of the work of medieval glaziers; we regret that there is so little of this beautiful craftsmanship remaining.

The Prior's Door was the entrance through which the Prior entered the Cathedral for worship from what is now the Deanery. Its stonework was recently cleaned and restored, and it shows all the detail of which both medieval masons were – and their modern successors are – capable. The Prior was a major

Above left ~ Stained glass, originally from the Cloisters
Above right ~ Roof boss from the Cloisters
Left ~ The Prior's Door

studying, the monks would retire to the Monks' Dormitory, the original ceiling of which may be seen below. Each roof beam was constructed from a single oak tree. The monks would have had little time to meditate on this; after an evening meal in the nearby Refectory, their duties during the day would have left them keen to sleep – especially as the service of Matins was said at midnight, and Lauds just before sunrise.

Above ~ The Cloisters
Above right ~ The West Towers seen from the Cloisters
Right ~ The ceiling of the Monks' Dormitory

figure in the life of the city, second in honour only to the Bishop, who was very powerful indeed. He would entertain any important personages who passed through Durham, including royalty. The expense of such a social role was considerable, but the wealth of the Priory was such that it could sustain this lifestyle. Such wealth inevitably added to the Prior's social status; however, Deans of Durham now enter the Cathedral through the same doors as their colleagues.

At the end of a day fully occupied with praying, eating, working around the monastery and

In the exhibition of the Treasures of St Cuthbert are displayed a number of the Cathedral's possessions relating to Cuthbert and the life of the Cathedral. Opposite is a general view from the entrance. A separate *Guide to the Treasures* is available; suffice it to say here that the exhibition is arranged in three sections, going back in time. The first represents the life of the Cathedral since the Reformation; the second shows something of its life as a medieval monastery; and the third displays items from the time of Cuthbert himself.

Chief among the exhibits are the remains of the coffin in which Cuthbert's body was placed in 698, and the pectoral cross that was not found until the tomb was excavated in 1827.

The flagon above is part of the collection of Dean and Chapter plate that was made in the eighteenth century. It is silver gilt, and engraved with the arms of Bishop John Cosin and the Diocese of Durham. This collection of silver is used for Holy Communion services in the Cathedral at ordinations and major festivals.

Above ~ Eighteenth-century silver-gilt flagon
Right ~ A capital letter from Hugh de Puiset's Bible

Left ~ Title page of St John's Gospel, from the seventh-century Durham Gospels
Middle left ~ A typical example of an illuminated missal (service book) from the Middle Ages

The Cathedral has a large collection of books, manuscripts and seals.

Gifts to the shrine, many of which were removed by the King's Commissioners at the Reformation, included the Lindisfarne Gospels, which are now in the British Library in London. The embroidery shown here is of a tenth-century stole. It was given to the shrine by King Athelstan in 934.

Above ~ Bishop Hatfield's Great Seal, 1378

Above ~ The Treasures of St Cuthbert
Right ~ Tenth-century embroidery
Below ~ The remains of St Cuthbert's Coffin

The Cathedral has always played its part in the life of the city and the county, and never more so than today. Around the annual commemoration of St Cuthbert's death, people come from a large number of parishes dedicated to him throughout the north-east. At the end of the service the whole congregation gathers in the Chapel of the Nine Altars, near his shrine, for the final prayers and blessing.

Many of the services in the Cathedral are sung by the Cathedral Choir; the choristers all attend the Chorister School, which provides day or boarding education for boys and girls from the ages of four to thirteen. Naturally a strong emphasis is placed on music, but not to the exclusion of other skills and fields of study.

Above ~ St Cuthbert service
Right ~ The Choir in procession

Above ~ The Nave as film set
Right ~ The Chapter House

Occasionally the Cathedral is used for filming. Our picture shows the Nave with all the pews removed for the filming of *Elizabeth*, which starred Cate Blanchett in the title role. The absence of seating makes it possible to see the full extent of the building. In a strange way it has the effect of bringing the building together so that the unity of its construction may be observed.

The view of the Chapter House provides a rare

glimpse into a part of the Cathedral complex that is not normally open to the public. It was originally built in the early twelfth century and was the place where the monks met to discuss their formal business of the monastery and hear a 'chapter' of the *Rule of St Benedict* read aloud – hence the name. This practice gave its name not only to the Chapter House but also to the group of people who met there – the 'Chapter' of the Cathedral.

The view of the Pulpit tells of the importance of preaching in Christian worship. It is a large

Above ~ The Pulpit seen from the North Aisle

construction, as befits a building of this size. Many would testify to its capacity to dwarf the speaker – and that is no bad thing, since they are not supposed to be concerned with promoting themselves, but rather with preaching the good news of Jesus Christ.

The masonry is worked in the Cathedral's works yard, where masons, joiners, electricians and plumbers all have a role in maintaining the fabric of the building and assisting in the constructive development of its beauty. In addition, the groundsmen keep the gardens stocked with flowers and the lawns in trim and attractive.

Left ~ Children examining sculpture
Below ~ A school party next to the Pulpit

Of the half-million visitors who come to Durham each year, twenty thousand are schoolchildren. Some of the education authorities in the region require a visit to Durham Cathedral as part of the National Curriculum in either Religious Knowledge or History. And there is much to see! Some children enjoy discovering the images of animals to be found here; others are impressed by the mathematics of the building; yet others are interested in its antiquity, and the fact that the oldest things in Durham Cathedral are the fossils that form part of the 'Frosterley Marble' in some of the stonework.

Left ~ The Cathedral Bookshop in the former Great Kitchen

Left ~ Cathedral masons at work
Below ~ Sculpture in the Masons' Yard

A team of cleaners ensures that the building remains presentable, both for those who work here and for those who visit.

Altogether, including the chorister school, the Cathedral provides employment for over one hundred people – and that does not include those businesses that supply the goods to keep the whole operation running.

The Bookshop is situated in what used to be the Great Kitchen of the Priory. It was built around 1340 and it was in use until 1940. Since 1997 it has housed the Cathedral Bookshop, which stocks a wide selection of theological books, as well as memorabilia of Durham and the region.

The Undercroft Restaurant, located in what was the Priory's Great Cellar or Buttery, is situated just off the Cloisters.

Above ~ A Cathedral joiner at work
Right ~ Cleaning the Lectern

The musical tradition at Durham is one of the finest in the land. The Organist and Master of the Choristers is assisted by a Sub-Organist, and there is also an Organ Scholar. The choristers and gentlemen of the Choir practise every day, and their commitment and skill are shown to good effect, not only on the great occasions such as Christmas, Easter and special services throughout the year, but also in the daily singing of Evensong and the regular worship of the Cathedral community on Sundays.

The Organ was built by Father Willis in 1876, rebuilt in 1905 and enlarged in 1935 by the local firm of Harrison and Harrison, who maintain it to this day. The ornate case and gilded organ pipes add to the beauty of the Quire, just as the instrument enhances daily worship.

Above ~ Choir practice
Left ~ The Organ in the Quire

The eighth-century manuscript on the left shows David playing a harp; it illustrates the significance of music in the life of the Church from early days.